THE SECRET DOOR TO SUCCESS

FLORENCE SCOVEL SHINN

CLASSY
PUBLISHING

THE SECRET DOOR TO SUCCESS
by Florence Scovel Shinn
Published by Classy Publishing, 2025

www.classypublishing.com
info@classypublishing.com

ISBN: 978-93-5522-444-6

For more books
Please visit *classypublishing.com*

CONTENTS

THE SECRET DOOR TO SUCCESS

> "So the people shouted when the priests blew with the trumpets: and it came to pass, when the people heard the sound of the trumpet, and the people shouted with a great shout, that the wall fell down flat, so that the people went up into the city, every man straight before him, and they took the city."—Joshua 6:20.

A successful man is always asked - "What is the secret of your success?"

People never ask a man who is a failure, "What is the secret of your failure?" It is quite easy to see and they are not interested.

People all want to know how to open the secret door of success.

For each man there is success, but it seems to be behind a door or wall. In the Bible reading, we have heard the wonderful story of the falling of the walls of Jericho.

Of course all biblical stories have a metaphysical interpretation.

We will talk now about *your* wall of Jericho: the wall separating *you* from *success*. Nearly everyone has built a wall around his own Jericho.

This city you are not able to enter, contains great treasures; your divinely designed success, your heart's desire!

What kind of wall have you built around your Jericho? Often, it is a wall of resentment—resenting someone, or resenting a situation, shuts off your good.

If you are a failure and resent the success of someone else, you are keeping away your own success.

I have given the following statement to neutralize envy and resentment.

What God has done for others, He now does for me and more.

A woman was filled with envy because a friend had received a gift, she made this statement, and an exact duplicate of the gift was given her—plus another present.

It was when the children of Israel shouted, that the walls of Jericho fell down. When you make an affirmation of Truth, your wall of Jericho totters.

I gave the following statement to a woman: *The walls of lack and delay now crumble away, and I enter my Promised Land, under grace.* She had a vivid picture of stepping over a fallen wall, and received the demonstration of her good, almost immediately.

It is the word of realization which brings about a change in your affairs; for words and thoughts are a form of radio-activity.

Taking an interest in your work, enjoying what you are doing opens the secret door to success.

A number of years ago I went to California to speak at the different centers, by way of the Panama Canal, and on the boat I met a man named Jim Tully.

For years he had been a tramp. He called himself The King of the Hoboes.

He was ambitious and picked up an education.

He had a vivid imagination and commenced writing stories about his experiences.

He dramatized tramp life, he enjoyed what he was doing, and became a very successful author. I remember one book called "Outside Looking In." It was made into a motion picture.

He is now famous and prosperous and lives in Hollywood. What opened the secret door to success for Jim Tully?

Dramatizing his life—being interested in what he was doing, he made the most of being a tramp. On the boat, we all sat at the captain's table, which gave us a chance to talk.

Mrs. Grace Stone was also a passenger on the boat; she had written the "Bitter Tea of General Yen," and was going to Hollywood to have it made into a moving-picture: she had lived in China and was inspired to write the book.

That is the *Secret* of Success, to *make what you are doing interesting to other people*. Be interested yourself, and others will find you interesting.

A good disposition, a smile, often opens the secret door; the Chinese say, "A man without a smiling face, must not open a shop."

The success of a smile was brought out in a French moving-picture in which Chevalier took the lead, the picture was called, "With a Smile." One of the characters had become poor, dreary and almost a derelict; He said to Chevalier "What good has my honesty done me?" Chevalier replied, "Even honesty won't help you, without a smile:" so the man changes on the spot, cheers up, and becomes very successful.

Living in the past, complaining of your misfortunes, builds a thick wall around your Jericho.

Talking too much about your affairs, scattering your forces, brings you up against a high wall. I knew a man of brains and ability, who was a complete failure.

He lived with his mother and aunt, and I found that every night when he went home to dinner, he told them all that had taken place during the day at the office; he discussed his hopes, his fears, and his failures.

I said to him, "You scatter your forces by talking about your affairs. Don't discuss your business with your family. Silence is Golden!"

He took my lead. During dinner he refused to talk about business, His mother and aunt were in despair: They loved to hear all about everything; but his silence proved golden!

Not long after, he was given a position at one hundred dollars a week, and in a few years, he had a salary of three hundred dollars a week.

Success is not a secret, it is a System.

Many people are up against the wall of discouragement. Courage and endurance are part of the system. We read this in lives of all successful men and women.

I had an amusing experience which brought this to my notice. I went to a moving picture theatre to meet a friend.

While waiting, I stood near a young boy, selling programs.

He called to people passing, "Buy a complete program of the picture, containing photographs of the actors and a sketch of their lives."

Most people passed by without buying. To my great surprise, he suddenly turned to me, and said - "Say, this ain't no racket for a guy with ambition!"

Then he gave a discourse on success. He said, "Most people give up just before something big is coming to them. A successful man never gives up.

Of course I was interested and said, "I'll bring you a book the next time I come. It is called *The Game of Life and How to Play It*. You will agree with a lot of the ideas."

A week or two later I went back with the book.

The girl at the ticket office said to him - "Let me read it, Eddie, while you are selling programs." The man who took tickets leaned over to see what it was about.

"The Game of Life" always gets people's interest.

I returned to the theatre in about three weeks, Eddie had gone. He had expanded into a new job that he liked. His wall of Jericho had crumbled, he had refused to be discouraged.

Only twice, is the word *success* mentioned in the Bible—both times in the Book of Joshua.

"Only be strong and very courageous to observe to do according to all the law which Moses, my servant, commanded thee: turn not from it to the right nor to the left, that thou mayest have good success whithersoever thou goest. This book of the law shall not depart from thy mouth, but thou shalt meditate therein day and night, that thou mayest observe to do all that is written therein, for then shalt thou make thy way prosperous and thou shalt have good success. Turn not to the right nor to the left."

The *road to success* is a *straight and narrow path; it is a road of loving absorption, of undivided attention.*

"You attract the things you give a great deal of thought to."

So if you give a great deal of thought to lack, you attract lack, if you give a great deal of thought to injustice, you attract more injustice.

Joshua said, "And it shall come to pass, that when they make a long blast with the ram's horn, and when ye hear the sound of the trumpet, all the people shall shout with a great shout: and the wall of the city shall fall down flat, and the people shall ascend up, every man straight before him."

The inner meaning of this story, is the power of the word, your word which dissolves obstacles, and removes barriers.

When the people shouted the walls fell down.

We find in folk-lore and fairy stories, which come down from legends founded on Truth, the same idea—a word opens a door or cleaves a rock.

We have it again in the Arabian Night's Story, "Ali Baba and The Forty Thieves." I saw it made into a moving picture.

Ali Baba has a secret hiding place, hidden somewhere behind rocks and mountains, the entrance may only be gained by speaking a secret word.—It is "Open Sesame!"

Ali Baba faces the mountain and cries - "Open Sesame!" and the rocks slide apart.

It is very inspiring, for it gives you the realization of how YOUR own rocks and barriers, *will part at the right word.*

So let us now take the statement—The walls of lack and delay now crumble away, and I enter my Promised Land, under grace.

BRICKS WITHOUT STRAW

"There shall no straw be given you, yet ye shall make bricks without straw."—Exodus 5:18.

In the 5th chapter of Exodus, we have a picture of every day life, when giving a metaphysical interpretation.

The Children of Israel were in bondage to Pharaoh, the cruel taskmaster, ruler of Egypt. They were kept in slavery, making bricks, and were hated and despised.

Moses had orders from the Lord to deliver his people from bondage - "Moses and Aaron went in and told Pharaoh—Thus saith the Lord God of Israel, Let my people go, that they may hold a feast unto me in the wilderness."

He not only refused to let them go, but told them he would make their tasks even more difficult: they must make bricks without straw being provided for them.

"And the task-masters of the people went out, and their officers, and they spake to the people, saying, Thus saith Pharaoh, I will not give you straw."

"Go ye, get you straw where ye can find it: yet not ought of your work shall be diminished."

It was impossible to make bricks without straw. The Children of Israel were completely crushed by Pharaoh, they were beaten for not producing the bricks—Then came the message from Jehovah.

"Go therefore now, and work; for there shall no straw be given you, yet shall ye deliver the tale (number) of bricks."

Working with Spiritual law they could make bricks without straw, which means to accomplish the seemingly impossible.

How often in life people are confronted with this situation.

Agnes M. Lawson in her "Hints to Bible Students" says - "The Life in Egypt under foreign oppression is the symbol of man under the hard taskmasters of Destructive thinking, Pride, Fear, Resentment, Ill-will, etc. The deliverance under Moses is the freedom man gains from the taskmasters, as he learns the law of life, for we can never come under grace, except we first know the law. The law must be made known in order to be fulfilled."

In the 111th Psalm we read in the final verse, "The fear of the Lord (law) is the beginning of Wisdom: a good understanding have all they that do his commandments: his praise endureth forever."

Now if we read the word Lord (law) it will give us the key to the statement.

The fear of the law (Karmic law) is the beginning of wisdom (not the fear of the Lord).

When we know that whatever we send out comes back, we begin to be afraid of our own boomerangs.

I read in a medical journal the following facts telling of the Boomerang this great Pharaoh received.

"It would appear that flesh is indeed heir to a long and ancient line of ills, when, as was revealed by Lord Monyahan at a lecture at Leeds, that the Pharaoh of the oppression suffered from hardening of the heart in a literal sense; Lord Monyahan showed some remarkable photographic slides of results of surgical operations a thousand years before Christ, and among these was a slide of the actual anatomical remains of the Pharaoh of the Oppression.

"The large vessel springing from the heart was in such a well-preserved state, as to enable sections of it to be made and compared with those made recently from the lantern slide. It was impossible to distinguish between the ancient and modern vessel. Both hearts had been attacked by Atheroma, a condition in which calcium salts are deposited in the walls of the vessel, making it rigid and inelastic.

"Inadequate expanse to the stream of blood from the heart caused the vessel to give way; with this condition went the mental changes that occur with a rigid arterial system: *A narrowness of outlook; restriction and dread of enterprise, a literal hardening of the heart.*"

So Pharaoh's hardness of heart, hardened his own heart.

This is as true today as it was several thousand years ago—we are all coming out of the Land of Egypt, out of the House of Bondage.

Your doubts and fears keep you in slavery; you face a situation which seems hopeless; What can you do? It is a case of making bricks without straw.

But remember the words of Jehovah, "Go therefore now, and work; for there shall no straw be given you, yet shall ye deliver the tale (number) of bricks."

You shall make bricks without straw. God makes a way where there is no way!

I was told the story of a woman who needed money for her rent: it was necessary to have it at once, she knew of no channel, she had exhausted every avenue.

However, she was a Truth student, and kept making her affirmations. Her dog whined and wanted to go out, she put on his leash and walked down the street, in the accustomed direction.

However, the dog pulled at his leash and wanted to go in another direction.

She followed, and in the middle of the block, opposite an open park, she looked down, and picked up a roll of bills, which exactly covered her rent.

She looked for ads, but never found the owner. There were no houses near where she found it.

The reasoning mind, the intellect, takes the throne of Pharaoh in your consciousness. It says continually, "It can't be done. What's the use!"

We must drown out these dreary suggestions with a vital affirmation!

For example take this statement: "*The unexpected happens, my seemingly impossible good now comes to pass.*" This stops all argument from the army of the aliens (the reasoning mind).

"The unexpected happens!" That is an idea it cannot cope with.

"Thou hast made me wiser than mine enemies." Your enemy thoughts, your doubts, fears and apprehensions!

Think of the joy of really being free forever, from the Pharaoh of the oppression. To have the idea of *security, health, happiness and abundance established in the subconscious.* It would mean a life free from all limitation!

It would be the Kingdom which Jesus Christ spoke of, where all things are automatically added unto us. I say automatically added unto us, because all life is vibration; and when we vibrate to success, happiness and abundance, the things which symbolize these states of consciousness will attach themselves to us.

Feel rich and successful, and suddenly you receive a large cheque or a beautiful gift.

I tell the story showing the working of this law. I went to a party where people played games, and whoever won, received a gift. The prize was a beautiful fan.

Among those present, was a very rich woman, who had everything. Her name was Clara. The poorer and resentful ones got together and whispered: "We hope Clara doesn't get the fan." Of course Clara won the fan.

She was care-free and vibrating to abundance. *Envy and resentment short-circuit your good* and keep away your fans.

If you should happen to be resentful and envious, take the statement; *What God has done for others He now does for me and more!*

Then all the fans and things will come your way.

No man gives to himself but himself, and no man takes away from himself but himself: the "Game of Life" is a game of solitaire; as you change, all conditions will change.

Now to go back to Pharaoh the oppressor; no one loves an oppressor.

I remember a friend I had many years ago, her name was Lettie; her father had plenty of money and supplied her mother and herself with food and clothes, but no luxuries.

We went to Art School together, and all the students would buy reproductions of the "Winged Victory," "Whistler's Mother" or something to bring art into their homes.

My friend's father called all these things "plunder." He would say, "Don't bring home any plunder."

So she lived a colorless life without a "Winged Victory" on her bureau or "Whistler's Mother" on the wall.

He would say often to my friend and her mother, "When I die, you'll both be well off."

One day someone said to Lettie, "When are you going abroad?" (all art students went abroad.)

She replied, cheerfully, "Not 'till Papa dies."

So people always look forward to being free from lack and oppression.

Let us now free ourselves from the *tyrants of negative thinking*: we have been slaves to doubts, fears and apprehension and let us be delivered as Moses delivered the Children of Israel; and come out of the Land of Egypt, out of the House of Bondage.

Find the thought which is your great oppressor; find the *King-Pin*.

In the logging camps in the Spring, the logs are sent down the rivers in great numbers.

Sometimes the logs become crossed and cause a jam; the men look for the log causing the jam (they call it the King-Pin), straighten it, and the logs rush down the river again.

Maybe your King-Pin is resentment, resentment holds back your good.

The more you resent, the more you will have to resent; you grow a resentment track in your brain, and your expression will be one of habitual resentment.

You will be avoided and miss the golden opportunities which await you each day.

I remember a few years ago, the streets were filled with men selling apples.

They got up early to get the good corners.

I passed one several times on Park Avenue, he had the most disagreeable expression I have ever seen.

As people passed he said, "Apples! Apples!" but no one stopped to buy.

I invested in an apple and said, "You'll never sell apples unless you change your expression."

He replied, "Well that guy over there took my corner."

I said, "Never mind about the corner, you can sell apples right here if you'll look pleasant."

He said "O. K. lady," and I went on. The next day I saw him, his whole expression had changed; he was doing a big business, selling apples with a smile.

So find your King-Pin—(you may have more than one); and your logs of *success, happiness and abundance will go rushing down your river.*

"Go therefore now and work, for there shall no straw be given you, yet ye shall make bricks without straw."

"AND FIVE OF THEM WERE WISE"

> "And five of them were wise, and five were foolish. They that were foolish took their lamps, and took no oil with them"—Math. 25:2:3.

My subject is the parable of the Wise and the Foolish Virgins. "And five of them were wise, and five were foolish. They that were foolish took their lamps, and took no oil with them. But the wise took oil in their vessels with their lamps." The parable teaches that true prayer means preparation.

Jesus Christ said, "And all things, whatsoever ye shall ask in prayer, *believing*, ye shall receive" (Math. 21:22). "Therefore I say unto you, what things soever ye desire, when ye pray, believe that ye receive them, and ye shall have them" (Mark 11:24). In this parable he shows that only those who have prepared for their good (thereby showing active faith) will bring the manifestation to pass.

We might paraphrase the scriptures and say: When ye pray believe ye have it. When ye pray ACT as if you have already received.

Armchair faith or rocking chair faith, will never move mountains. In the armchair, in the silence, or meditation, you are filled with the wonder of this Truth, and feel that your faith will never waver. You know that The Lord is your Shepherd, you shall never want.

You feel that your God of Plenty will wipe out all burdens of debt or limitations. Then you leave your armchair and step out into the arena of Life. It is only what you do in the arena that counts.

I will give you an illustration showing how the law works; for faith without action is dead.

A man, one of my students, had a great desire to go abroad. He took the statement: *I give thanks for my divinely designed trip, divinely financed, under grace, in a perfect way.* He had very little money, but knowing the law of preparation, he bought a trunk. It was a very gay and happy trunk with a big red band around its waist. Whenever he looked at it it gave him a realization of a trip. One day he seemed to feel his room moving. He felt the motion of a ship. He went to the window to breathe the fresh air, and it smelt like the aroma of the docks. With his inner ear he heard the shriek of a sea-gull and the creaking of the gangplank. The trunk had commenced to work. It had put him in the vibration of his trip. Soon after that, a large sum of money came to him and he took the trip. He said afterwards that it was perfect in every detail.

In the arena of Life we must keep ourselves tuned-up to concert pitch.

Are we acting from motives of fear or faith? *Watch your motives with all diligence, for out of them are the issues of life.*

If your problem is a financial one (and it usually is), you must know how to wind yourself up financially, and keep wound up by always acting your faith. The material attitude towards money is to trust in your salary, your income and investments, which can shrink over night.

The spiritual attitude toward money is to trust in God for your supply. To keep your possessions, always realize that they are God in manifestation. "What Allah has given cannot be diminished," then if one door shuts another door, immediately, opens.

Never voice lack or limitation for "by your words you are condemned." You combine with what you notice, and if you are always noticing failure and hard times, you will combine with failure and hard times.

You must form the habit of living in the fourth dimension, "The World of the Wondrous." It is the world where you do not judge by appearances.

You have trained your inner eye to see through failure into success, to see through sickness into health to see through limitation into plenty. I will give you the land which your inner eye sees. "I will give to you the land which thou seeth."

The man who achieves success has the *fixed idea of success.* If it is founded on a rock of truth and rightness it will stand. If not, it is built upon sand and washed into the sea, returning to its native nothingness.

Only divine ideas can endure. Evil destroys itself, for it is a cross current against universal order, and the way of the transgressor is hard.

"They that were foolish took their lamps, and took no oil with them. But the wise took oil in their vessels with their lamps."

The lamp symbolizes man's consciousness. The oil is what brings Light or understanding.

"While the bridegroom tarried, they all slumbered and slept. And at midnight there was a cry made, Behold, the bridegroom cometh; go ye out to meet him. Then all those virgins arose, and trimmed their lamps. And the foolish said unto the wise, Give us your oil; for our lamps are gone out."

The foolish virgins were without wisdom or understanding, which is oil for the consciousness, and when they were confronted with a serious situation, they had no way of handling it.

And when they said to the wise "give us of your oil," the wise answered saying, "Not so; lest there be not enough for us and you: but go ye rather to them that sell, and buy for yourselves."

That means that the foolish virgins could *not receive more than was in their consciousness*, or what they were vibrating to.

The man received the trip because it was in his consciousness, as a reality. He believed that he had already received. As he prepared for the trip he was taking oil for his lamps. With *realization comes manifestation*.

The law of preparation works both ways. If you prepare for what you fear or don't want, you begin to attract it. David said, "The thing I feared has come upon me." We hear people say, "I must put away money in case of illness." They are deliberately preparing to be ill. Or, "I'm saving for a rainy day." The rainy day is sure to come, at a most inconvenient time.

The divine idea for every man is plenty. Your barns *should be* full, and your cup *should* flow over, but we must learn to ask aright.

For example take this statement: *I call on the law of accumulation. My supply comes from God, and now pours in and piles up, under grace.*

This statement does not give any picture of stint or saving or sickness. It gives a fourth dimensional feeling of abundance, leaving the channels to Infinite Intelligence.

Every day you must make a choice, will you be wise or foolish? Will you prepare for your good? Will you *take the giant swing into faith?* Or serve doubt and fear and bring no oil for your lamps?

"And while they went to buy, the bridegroom came; and they that were ready went in with him to the marriage: and the door was shut. Afterward came also the other virgins, saying, Lord, Lord, open to us. But he answered and said, Verily I say unto you, I know you not."

You may feel that the foolish virgins paid very dearly for neglecting to bring oil for their lamps, but we are dealing with the law of Karma (or the law of come back). It has been called the "judgement day," which people usually associate with the end of the world.

Your judgement day comes, they say, in sevens—seven hours, seven days, seven weeks, seven months, or seven years. It might even come in seven minutes. Then you pay some Karmic debt; the price for having violated spiritual law. *You failed to trust God, you took no oil for your lamps.*

Every day examine your consciousness and see just what you are preparing for. You are fearful of lack and hang on to every cent, thereby attracting more lack. Use what you have with wisdom and it opens the way for more to come to you.

In my book, "Your Word Is Your Wand," I tell about the Magic Purse. In the Arabian Nights they tell the story of a man who had a Magic Purse. As money went out, immediately money appeared in it again.

So I made the statement. *My supply comes from God—I have the magic purse of the spirit. It can never be depleted. As money goes out, immediately money comes in. It is always crammed, jammed with abundance, under grace, in perfect ways.*

This brings a vivid picture to mind: You are drawing on the bank of the imagination.

A woman who did not have much money was afraid to pay any bills and see her bank account dwindle. It came to her with great conviction: "I have the magic purse of the spirit. It can never be depleted. As money goes out, immediately, money comes in." She fearlessly paid her bills, and several large cheques came to her that she did not expect.

"Watch and pray lest ye enter into the temptation" of preparing for something destructive instead of something constructive.

I knew a woman who told me she always kept a long crepe veil handy in case of funerals. I said to her, "You are a menace to your relatives, and are preparing to hurry them all off, so that you can wear the veil." She destroyed it.

Another woman who had no money decided to send her two daughters to college. Her husband scorned the idea and said, "Who will pay their tuition? I have no money for it." She replied, "I know some *unforeseen good will come to us*." She kept on preparing her daughters for college. Her husband laughed heartily and told all their friends that his wife was sending the girls to college on "some unforeseen good." A rich relative suddenly sent her a large sum of money. "Some unforeseen good" *did* arrive, for she had shown active faith. I asked what she had said to her husband when the cheque arrived. She replied, "Oh, I never antagonize George by telling him I am in the right."

So prepare for your "unforeseen good." Let every thought and every act express your unwavering faith. Every event in your life is a crystallized idea. Something you have invited through either fear or faith. *Something you have prepared for.*

So let us be wise and bring oil for our lamps—and when we least expect it, we shall reap the fruits of our faith.

My lamps are now filled with the oil of faith and fulfillment.

WHAT DO YOU EXPECT?

According to your faith be it unto you.—Matt. 9:29

Faith is expectancy, "According to your faith, be it unto you."

We might say, according to your expectancies be it done unto you; so, what are you expecting?

We hear people say: "We expect the worst to happen," or "The worst is yet to come." They are deliberately inviting the worst to come.

We hear others say: "I expect a change for the better." They are inviting better conditions into their lives.

Change your expectancies and you change your conditions.

How can you change your expectancies, when you have formed the habit of expecting loss, lack or failure?

Begin to act as if you *expected* success, happiness and abundance; *prepare for your good.*

Do something to show you expect it to come. Active faith alone, will impress the subconscious.

If you have spoken the word for a home, prepare for it immediately, as if you hadn't a moment to lose. Collect little ornaments, table-cloths, etc. etc.!

I knew a woman who made the giant swing into faith, by buying a large arm-chair; a chair meant business, she bought a large and comfortable chair, for she was preparing for the right man. He came.

Someone will say, "Suppose you haven't money to buy ornaments or a chair?" Then look in shop windows and link with them in thought.

Get in their vibration: I sometimes hear people say; "I don't go into the shops because I can't afford to buy anything." That is just the reason you should go into the shops. Begin to make friends with the things you desire or require.

I know a woman who wanted a ring. She went boldly to the ring department and tried on rings.

It gave her such a realization of ownership, that not long after, a friend made her a gift of a ring. "You combine with what you notice."

Keep on noticing beautiful things, and you make an invisible contact. Sooner or later these things are drawn into your life, unless you say, "Poor me, too good to be true."

"My soul, wait thou only upon God: for my expectation is from Him." This is a most important statement from the 62nd Psalm.

The soul is the subconscious mind, and the psalmist was telling his subconscious to expect everything directly from the universal; not to depend upon doors and channels; "My expectation is from Him."

God cannot fail, for "His ways are ingenious, His methods are sure."

You can expect any seemingly impossible Good from God; if you do not limit the channels.

Do not say how you want it done, or how it can't be done.

"God is the Giver and the Gift *and creates His own amazing channels*."

Take the following statement: *I cannot be separated from God the Giver, therefore, I cannot be separated from God the Gift. The gift is God in action.*

Get the realization that every blessing is *Good in action*, and see God in every face and good in every situation: This makes you master of all conditions.

A woman came to me saying that there was no heat in the radiators in their apartment, and that her mother was suffering from the cold. She added, "The landlord has declared that we can't have heat until a certain date:" I replied, "God is your landlord." She said, "That's all I want to know," and rushed out. That evening the heat was turned on without asking. It was because she realized that the landlord was God in manifestation.

This is a wonderful age, for people are becoming Miracle Minded; it is in the air.

Quoting from an article which I found in the New York Journal and American by John Anderson, it corroborates what I have just said.

The title of the article is "Theatre Goers Make Hits of Metaphysical Plays."

If, said a cynical manager, who shall be called Brock Pemberton, with a slight accent of sarcasm in his voice, the other night, on an intermission curbside talk, you fellows, meaning the critics, know so much about what the New York public wants, why don't you tell me what to produce? Why don't you run me into business instead of out of it? "Why don't you tell me what sort of play the play-goers want to see?" "I would," I said, "But you wouldn't believe it."

"You're hedging," he said, "You don't know, and you're trying to cover up by pretending to know more than you're willing to say. You haven't any more idea than I have this minute what sort of plays generally succeed."

"I have," I said, "there is one sure fire success; one theme that works and has always worked, whether it is competing with boy meets girl, mysteries, historical tragedies, etc.; no play on the theme has ever completely failed if it had any merit at all, and a lot of poor ones have been big hits."

"You're stalling again," said Mr. Pemberton, "What sort of plays are they?"

"Metaphysical," I said, fouling slightly with a big word and waiting quietly for the effect. "Metaphysical," said Mr. Pemberton, "You mean metaphysical?"

I paused a moment and since Mr. Pemberton said nothing, went right on spouting such titles as "The Green Pastures," "The Star Wagon," "Father Malachy's Miracle!, etc." "Some of these," I added, "reached the public *over* the heads of the critics." But Mr. Pemberton had departed to ask probably, in every theatre in town, "Is there a metaphysician in the house?"

People are beginning to realize the power of their words and thoughts. They understand why "Faith *is* the substance of the thing hoped for, the evidence of things not seen."

We see the law of expectancy working out through superstition.

If you walk under a ladder and expect it to give you bad luck, it will give you bad luck. The ladder is quite innocent; bad luck came because you expected it.

We might say, expectancy is the substance of the things hoped for; or expectancy is the substance of the thing man fears; "The thing I expected has come upon me."

Nothing as too good to be true, nothing is too wonderful to happen, nothing is too good to last; when you look to God for your good.

Now think of the blessings which seem so far off, and begin to expect them now, under grace, in an unexpected way; for God works in unexpected ways, His wonders to perform.

I was told that there are three thousand promises in the Bible.

Let us now expect all these blessings to come to pass. Among them we are promised Riches and Honor, Eternal Youth ("Your flesh shall become as a little child's) and Eternal Life, "death itself shall be overcome."

Christianity as founded upon the forgiveness of sins and an empty tomb.

We now know that all these things are scientifically possible.

As we call on the law of forgiveness, we become free from mistakes and the consequences of mistakes. ("Though your sins be as scarlet ye shall be washed whiter than wool.")

Then our bodies will be bathed in Light, and express the "body electric," which is incorruptible and indestructible, pure substance, expressing perfection.

I expect the unexpected, my glorious good now comes to pass.

THE LONG ARM OF GOD

"The Eternal God is thy refuge, and underneath are the everlasting arms."—Deut. 33:27

In the bible, the arm of God always symbolizes protection. The writers of the bible knew the power of a symbol. It brings a picture which impresses the subconscious mind. They used the symbols of the rock, sheep, shepherds, vineyard, lamp, and hundreds of others. It would be interesting to know how many symbols are used in the bible. The arm also symbolizes strength.

"The eternal God is thy refuge, and underneath are the everlasting arms: and he shall thrust out the enemy from before thee; and shall say, Destroy them."

Who is the enemy "before thee." The negative thought-forms which you have built up in your subconscious mind. A man's enemies are only those of his own household. The everlasting arms thrust out these enemy thoughts and destroy them.

Have you ever felt the relief of getting out some negative thought-form? Perhaps you have built up a thought-form of resentment, until you are always boiling with anger about something. You resent people you know, people you don't know—people in the past and people in the present; and you may be sure that the people in the future won't escape your wrath.

All the organs of the body are affected by resentment—for when you resent, you resent with every organ of the body. You pay the penalty with rheumatism, arthritis, neuritis, etc., for acid thoughts produce acid in the blood. All this trouble comes because you are fighting the battle, not leaving it to the long arm of God.

I have given the following statement to many of my students. *The long arm of God reaches out over people and conditions, controlling this situation and protecting my interests.*

This brings a picture of a long arm symbolizing strength and protection. With the realization of the power of the long arm of God, you would no longer resist or resent. You would relax and let go. The enemy thoughts within you would be destroyed, therefore, *the adverse conditions would disappear.*

Spiritual development means the ability to stand still, or stand aside, and let Infinite Intelligence lift your burdens and fight your battles. When the burden of resentment is lifted, you experience a sense of relief! You have a kindly feeling for everyone, and all the organs of your body begin to function properly.

A clipping quoting Albert Edward Day, D.D. reads, "That loving our enemies is good for our spiritual health is widely known and accepted. But that negation and poisonous emotions destroy physical health, is a relatively new discovery. The problem of health is often an emotional one. Wrong emotions entertained and repeated are potent causes of illness. When the preacher talks about loving your enemies, the man on the street is apt to dismiss the idea as unendurable and pious. But the fact is, the preacher is telling you something which is one of the first laws of hygiene, as well as ethics. No man even for his body's sake can afford to indulge in hatred. It is like repeated doses of poison. When you are urged to get rid of fear, you are not listening to a moon-struck idealist; rather you are hearing counsel that is as significant for health as advice about diet."

We hear so much about a balanced diet, but without a balanced mind you can't digest what you eat, calories or no calories.

Non-resistance is an art. When acquired, The World is Yours! So many people are trying to force situations. Your lasting good will never come through forcing personal will.

> "Flee from the things which flee from thee,
> Seek nothing, fortune seeketh thee.
> Behold his shadow on the floor!
> Behold him standing at the door!"

I do not know the author of these lines. Lovelock, the celebrated English athlete, was asked how to attain his speed and endurance in running. He replied, "Learn to relax." Let us attain this rest in action. He was most relaxed when running the fastest.

Your big opportunity and big success usually *slide in*, when you least expect it. You have to let go long enough for the *great law of attraction to operate. You never saw a worried and anxious magnet*. It stands up straight and hasn't a care in the world, because it knows the needles can't help jumping to it. The things we rightly desire come to pass when we have taken the clutch off.

I say in my correspondence course, "*Do not let your heart's desire become a heart's disease." You are completely demagnetized when you desire something too intensely.* You worry, fear, and agonize. There is an occult law of indifference: "None of these things move me." *Your ships come in over a don't care sea.*

Many people in Truth antagonize friends, because they are too anxious for them to read the books and go to the lectures. They meet opposition.

A friend took my book, "The Game of Life and How to Play It" to her brother's house to read. The young men of the family refused to read it. No "nut stuff" for them. One of these young men drives a taxi cab. One night he drove a taxi which belonged to another man. In going over the car he found a book stuffed away somewhere. It was "The Game of Life and How to Play It." The next day he said to his aunt, "I found Mrs. Shinn's book in the taxi last night. I read it and it's great! There's a lot of good reading in it. Why doesn't she write another book?" God works in roundabout ways, His wonders to perform.

I meet unhappy people and a few grateful and contented people. A man said to me one day, "I have a great deal to be thankful for. I have good health, enough money and I'm still single!"

The eighty-ninth psalm is very interesting, for we find that two individuals take part; the man who sings the psalm (for all psalms are songs or poems), and the Lord God of

Hosts answers him. It is a song of praise and thanksgiving, extolling the strong arm of God.

"I will sing of the mercies of the Lord forever!"

"O Lord God of Hosts, who is a strong Lord like unto thee?"

"Thou hast a mighty arm: strong is thy hand, and high is thy right hand."

Then the Lord of Hosts replies.

"With whom my hand shall be established: mine arm also shall strengthen him."

"My mercy will I keep for him for evermore, and my covenant shall stand fast with him."

We only hear the words "for evermore" in the bible and in fairy-tales. In the absolute, man is outside of time and space. His good is "from everlasting to everlasting." The fairy-tales came down from the old Persian legends which were founded upon Truth.

Aladdin and His Wonderful Lamp is the out-picturing of the Word. Aladdin rubbed the lamp and all his desires came to pass. Your word is your lamp. Words and thoughts are a form of radio activity and do not return void. A scientist has said that words are clothed in light. *You are continually reaping the fruits of your words.*

A friend in one of my meeting said that she had brought a man to my class who had been out of work for a year or more. I gave the statement: *Now is the appointed time. Today is the day of my amazing good fortune.* It clicked in his consciousness. Soon after, he was given a position which paid him nine thousand dollars a year.

A woman told me that when I blessed the offering I said that each offering would return a thousandfold. She had put a dollar in the collection. She said with great realization, "That dollar is blessed and returns a thousand dollars." She received a thousand dollars a short time afterwards, in a most unexpected way.

Why do some people demonstrate this Truth so much more quickly than others? It is because they have the ears that hear. Jesus Christ tells the parable of the man who sowed the seed and it fell upon good ground. The seed is the word. I say, "*Listen for the statement that clicks; the statement that gives you realization. That statement will bear fruit.*"

The other day I went into a shop where I know the employer quite well. I had given one of his employees an affirmation card. I said to him, jokingly, "I wouldn't waste an affirmation card on you. You wouldn't use it." He replied, "Oh, sure, give me one. I'll use it." The following week I gave him a card. Before I left he rushed up to me excitedly and said, "I made that statement and two new customers walked in." It was: "Now is the appointed time; today is the day of my amazing good fortune." It had clicked.

So many people use their words in exaggerated and reckless statements. I find a great deal of material for my talks in the beauty parlor. A young girl wanted a magazine to read. She called to the operator, "Give me something terribly new and frightfully exciting." All she wanted was the latest moving picture magazine. You hear people say, "I wish something terribly exciting would happen." They are inviting some unhappy, but exciting, experience into their lives. Then they wonder why it happened to them.

There should be a chair of metaphysics in all colleges. *Metaphysics is the wisdom of the ages.* It is the ancient wisdom taught all through the centuries in India and Egypt and Greece. Hermes Trismegistus was a great teacher of Egypt. His teachings were closely guarded and have come down to us over ten centuries. He lived in Egypt in the days when the present race of men was in its infancy. But if you read the "Kybalion" carefully, you will find that he taught just what we are teaching today. He said that all mental states were accompanied by vibrations. You combine with what you vibrate to, so let us all now vibrate to success, happiness and abundance.

Now is the appointed time. Today is the day of my amazing good fortune.

THE FORK IN THE ROAD

"Choose you this day whom ye will serve."—Josh. 24:15.

Every day there is a necessity of choice (a fork in the road).

"Shall I do this, or shall I do that? Shall I go, or shall I stay?" Many people do not know what to do. They rush about letting other people make decisions for them, then regret having taken their advice.

There are others who carefully reason things out. They weigh and measure the situation like dealing in groceries, and are surprised when they fail to attain their goal.

There are still other people who follow the magic path of intuition and find themselves in their Promised Land in the twinkling of an eye.

Intuition is a spiritual faculty high above the reasoning mind, but on that path is all that you desire or require.

In my book "The Game of Life and How to Play It," I give many examples of success attained through using this marvelous faculty. I say also that prayer is telephoning to God and intuition is God telephoning to you. (Correspondence Course.)

So choose ye this day to follow the magic path of intuition.

In my question and answer classes I tell you how to cultivate intuition.

In most people it is a faculty which has remained dormant. So we say, "Awake thou that sleepeth. Wake up to your leads and hunches. Wake up to the divinity within!"

Claude Bragdon said, "To live intuitively is to live fourth dimensionally."

Now it is necessary for you to make a decision, you face a fork in the road. *Ask for a definite unmistakable lead*, and you will receive it.

We find many events to interpret metaphysically in the Book of Joshua. "After the death of Moses, the divine command came to Joshua, 'Now therefore, arise, go over the Jordan, thou and all thy people, unto the land which I do give to them. Every place the sole of your feet shall tread upon; to you have I given it.'"

The feet are the symbol of understanding, so it means metaphysically all that we understand stands under us in consciousness, and what is rooted there can never be taken from us.

For, the bible goes on to say: "There shall not any man be able to stand before thee all the days of thy life. . . . I will not fail thee, nor forsake thee. Only be thou strong and very courageous, that thou mayest observe to do according to all the law, which Moses my servant commanded thee: turn not from it to the right hand or to the left, that thou mayest prosper whithersoever thou goest."

So we find we have success through being strong and very courageous in following spiritual law. We are back again to the "fork in the road"—the necessity of choice.

"Choose you this day whom ye will serve," the intellect or divine guidance.

A well-known man, who has become a great power in the financial world, said to a friend, "I always follow intuition and I am luck incarnate."

Inspiration (which is divine guidance) is the most important thing in life. People come to Truth meetings for inspiration. I find the right word will start divine activity operating in their affairs.

A woman came to me with a complication of affairs. I said to her, "Let God juggle the situation." It clicked. She took the affirmation, "I now let God juggle this situation." Almost immediately she rented a house, which had been vacant for a long time.

Let God juggle every situation, for when you try to juggle the situation, you drop all the balls.

In my question and answer classes, I would be asked, "How do you let God juggle a situation, and what do you mean when you say I should not juggle it?"

You juggle with the intellect. The intellect would say, "Times are hard, no activity in real estate. Don't expect anything until the Fall of 1958."

With spiritual law there is only the *now*. Before you call you are answered, for "time and space are but a dream," and *your blessing is there waiting for you to release it by faith and the word.*

"Choose you this day whom ye will serve," fear or faith.

In every act prompted by fear lies the germ of its own defeat.

It takes much strength and courage to trust God. We often trust him in little things, but when it comes to a big situation we feel we had better attend to it ourselves; then comes defeat and failure.

The following extract from a letter which I received from a woman in the West shows how conditions can change in the twinkling of an eye.

"I've had the pleasure of reading your wonderful book, The Game of Life and How to Play It.' I have four boys, ten, thirteen, fifteen and seventeen, and thought how wonderful for them to grasp it, in their early life, and be able to get things which are theirs by Divine Right.

"The lady who let me read her copy gave me other things to read, but it seemed when I picked this book up it was magnetic and I could not let go of it. After reading it I realized, I was trying to live Divinely but did not understand the law, or I would have been much further advanced.

"At first I thought it quite hard to find a place in the business world, after so many years of being a mother. But I got this statement, '*God makes a way where there is no way.*' And He did that very thing for me.

"I am grateful for my position, and smile when people say, 'How do you do it, manage four growing boys, a home, after all the times you have been hospitalized with such major operations, and none of your relatives near you?' "

I have that statement in my book, "*God makes a way where there is no way.*"

God made a way for her in business when all her friends said it couldn't be done.

The average person will tell you almost anything can't be done.

I had an example of this the other day. In a shop I found a delightful little silver dripolator which would make just one cup of anything. I showed it to some friends with enthusiasm, thinking it so very cute, and one said, "It will never work." The other said, "If it belonged to me, I'd throw it away." I stood up for the little dripolator and said I knew it would work, which it did.

My friends were simply typical of the average person who says, "It can't be done."

All big ideas meet with opposition.

Do not let other people rock your boat.

Follow the path of wisdom and understanding, "and turn not from it to the right hand or to the left, that thou mayest prosper whithersoever thou goest."

In the thirteenth verse of the twenty-fourth chapter of Joshua, we read a remarkable statement: "And I have given you a land for which ye did not labour, and cities which ye built not, and ye dwell in them; of the vineyards and oliveyards which ye planted not, do ye eat."

This shows that man cannot *earn* anything, his blessings come as gifts. (Gifts lest any man shall boast.)

With the *realization of wealth*, we receive the gift of wealth.

With the *realization of success*, we receive the gift of success, for success and abundance are states of mind.

"For it is the Lord our God, he it is, that brought us up, and our fathers out of the land of Egypt, out of the house of bondage."

The land of Egypt stands for darkness—the house of bondage, where man is a slave to his doubts and fears, and beliefs in lack and limitation, the result of having followed the wrong fork in the road.

Misfortune is due to failure to stick to the things which spirit has revealed through intuition.

All big things have been accomplished by men who stuck to their big ideas.

Henry Ford was past middle age when the idea of the Ford car came to him. He had great difficulty in raising the money. His friends thought it was a crazy idea. His father said to him, tearfully, "Henry, why do you give up a good twenty-five dollar a week job in order to chase a crazy idea?" But no one could rock Henry Ford's boat.

So in order to come out of the land of Egypt, out of the house of bondage, we must make the right decisions.

Follow the right fork in the road. "Only be thou strong and very courageous, that thou mayest observe to do according to the law, which Moses my servant commanded thee: turn not from it to the right hand nor to the left, that thou mayest prosper whithersoever thou goest."

So, as we reach the fork in the road today, let us fearlessly follow the voice of intuition.

The bible calls it "the still small voice."

"There came a voice behind me, saying, 'This is the way, walk ye in it.'"

On this path is the good, already prepared for you.

You will find the "land for which ye did not labour, and cities which ye built not, and ye dwell in them; of the vineyards and oliveyards which ye planted not, do ye eat."

I am divinely led, I follow the right fork in the road. God makes a way where there is no way.

CROSSING YOUR RED SEA

> "Speak unto the children of Israel that they go forward."
> Ex. 14:15

One of the most dramatic stories in the bible is the episode of the children of Israel crossing the Red Sea.

Moses was leading them out of the land of Egypt where they were kept in bondage and slavery. They were being pursued by the Egyptians.

The children of Israel, like most people, did not enjoy trusting God; they did a lot of murmuring. They said to Moses: "Is not this the word that we did tell thee in Egypt, saying, Let us alone, that we may serve the Egyptians? For it had been better for us to serve the Egyptians, than that we should die in the wilderness."

"And Moses said unto the people, Fear ye not, stand still, and see the salvation of the Lord, which he will show to you today: for the Egyptians whom ye have seen today, ye shall see them again no more for ever."

"The Lord shall fight for you, and ye shall hold your peace."

We might say that Moses pounded faith into the children of Israel.

They preferred being slaves to their old doubts and fears (for Egypt stands for darkness), than to take the giant swing into faith, and pass through the wilderness to their Promised Land.

There is, indeed, a wilderness to pass through before your Promised Land is reached.

The old doubts and fears encamp round about you, but, there is always someone to tell you to go forward! There is always a Moses on your pathway. Sometimes it is a friend, sometimes intuition!

"And the Lord said to Moses, Wherefore criest thou unto me? Speak unto the children of Israel, that *they go forward!*"

"But lift thou up thy rod, and stretch out thine hand over the sea, and divide it: and the children of Israel shall go on dry ground through the midst of the sea."

"And Moses stretched out his hand over the sea; and the Lord caused the sea to go back by a strong east wind all that night, and made the sea dry land, and the waters were divided."

"And the children of Israel went into the midst of the sea upon the dry ground: and the waters were a wall unto them on their right hand, and on their left."

"And the Egyptians pursued, and went in after them to the midst of the sea, even all Pharaoh's horses, his chariots, and his horsemen.

"And the Lord said unto Moses, Stretch out thine hand over the sea, that the waters may come again upon the Egyptians, upon their chariots, and upon their horsemen."

"And Moses stretched forth his hand over the sea, and the sea returned; and the Egyptians fled against it; and the Lord overthrew the Egyptians in the midst of the sea."

"And the waters returned, and covered the chariots, and the horsemen, and all the hosts of Pharaoh that came into the sea after them; there remained not so much as one of them."

Now remember, the bible is talking about the individual. It is talking about your wilderness, your Red Sea, and *your* Promised Land.

Each one of you has a Promised Land, a heart's desire, but you have been so enslaved by the Egyptians (your negative thoughts), it seems very far away, and too good to be true. You consider trusting God a very risky proposition. The wilderness might prove worse than the Egyptians.

And how do you know your Promised Land really exists?

The reasoning mind will always back up the Egyptians.

But sooner or later, something says, "*Go forward!*" It is usually circumstances—you are driven to it.

I give the example of a student.

She is a very marvelous pianist and had great success abroad. She came back with a book full of press clippings, and a happy heart.

A relative took an interest in her and said she would back her financially for a concert tour. They chose a manager who took charge of the expenses, and attended to her bookings.

After a concert or two, there were no more funds. The manager had taken them. My friend was left stranded, desolate and disappointed. This was about the time that she came to me.

She hated the man, and it was making her ill. She had very little money and could afford only a cheerless room where her hands were often too cold to practice.

She was indeed, in bondage to the Egyptians—hate, resentment, lack and limitation.

Someone brought her to one of my meetings, and she spoke to me and told her story.

I said, "In the first place you must stop hating that man. When you are able to forgive him, your success will come back to you. You are taking your initiation in forgiveness."

It seemed a pretty big order, but she tried and came regularly to all my meetings.

In the meantime, the relative had started a suit to recover the money. Time went on and it never came to court.

My friend had a call to go to California. She was no longer disturbed by the situation, and had forgiven the man.

Suddenly, after about four years, she was notified that the case had come to court. She called me upon her arrival in New York, and asked me to speak the word for rightness and justice.

They went at the time appointed, and it was all settled out of court, the man restoring the money by monthly payments.

She came to me overflowing with joy, for she said, "I hadn't the least resentment toward the man. He was amazed when I greeted him cordially." Her relative said that all the money was to go to her, so she found herself with a big bank account.

Now she will soon reach her Promised Land. She came out of the house of bondage (of hate and resentment) and crossed her red sea. Her goodwill toward the man caused the waters to part, and she crossed over on dry land.

Dry land symbolizes something substantial under your feet, the feet symbolizing understanding.

Moses stands out as one of the greatest figures in biblical history.

"It came to Moses to move from Egypt with his nation. The task before him was not only the unwillingness of Pharaoh to let go of those whom he had made into profitable slaves, but also to stimulate to open rebellion this nation which had lost its initiative under the hardships of its taskmasters."

"It required extraordinary genius to meet this condition, which Moses possessed with self abnegation and the courage of his own convictions. Self abnegation! He was called the meekest of men. We have often heard the expression, 'As meek as Moses.' He was so meek towards the commands of the Lord, that he became one of the strongest of men."

The Lord said to Moses, "lift thou up thy rod, and stretch out thine hand over the sea, and divide it: and the children of Israel shall go on dry ground through the midst of the sea."

So, never doubting, he said to the children of Israel, "Go forward." This was a daring thing to do, to lead a multitude of people into the sea, having perfect faith they would not drown.

Behold the miracle!

". . . the Lord caused the sea to go back by a strong east wind all that night, and made the sea dry land, and the waters were divided."

Now remember, this could happen *for you* this very day. Think of your problem.

Maybe you have lost your initiative from living so long a slave to Pharaoh—(your doubts, fears and discouragements).

Say to yourself, "*Go forward.*"

". . . the Lord caused the sea to go back by a strong east wind."

We will think of this strong east wind as a strong affirmation.

Take a vital statement of Truth. For example, if your problem is a financial one, say: "*My supply comes from God, and big happy financial surprises now come to me, under grace, in perfect ways.*" The statement is a good one, for it contains the element of mystery.

We are told that God works in mysterious ways His wonders to perform. We might say in surprising ways. Now that you have made your statement for supply, you have caused the east wind to blow.

So walk up to your Red Sea of lack or limitation. The way to walk up to your Red Sea is to do something to show your fearlessness.

I will tell the story of a student who had an invitation to visit friends at a very fashionable summer resort.

She had been living in the country for a long time, grown heavier, and nothing fitted her but her girl scout suit. Suddenly, she received the invitation. It meant evening clothes, slippers and accessories, none of which she had, and no money to buy them. She came to me. I said, "What is your hunch?"

She replied, "I feel very fearless. I have the hunch to go, anyway."

So she squeezed herself into something to travel in, and went.

When she arrived at her friend's house she was greeted warmly, but her hostess said, with some embarrassment, "Maybe what I've done will hurt you, but there are some evening clothes and slippers I never wear which I have put in your room. Won't you make use of them?"

My friend assured her she would be delighted—and everything fitted perfectly.

She had, indeed, walked up to her Red Sea and passed over on dry land.

The waters of my Red Sea part, and I pass over on dry land, I now go forward into my Promised Land.

THE WATCHMAN AT THE GATE

> "Also I set watchmen over you, saying, Hearken to the sound of the trumpet."—Jeremiah 6:17?

We must all have a watchman at the gate of our thoughts. The Watchman at the Gate is the superconscious mind.

We have the power to choose our thoughts.

Since we have lived in the race thought for thousands of years, it seems almost impossible to control them. They rush through our minds like stampeding cattle or sheep.

But a single sheep-dog can control the frightened sheep and guide them into the sheep pen.

I saw a picture in the news-reels of a shepherd-dog controlling the sheep. He had rounded up all but three. These three resisted and resented. They baahed and lifted their front feet in protest, but the dog simply sat down in front and never took his eyes off them. He did not bark or threaten. He just sat and looked his determination. In a little while the sheep tossed their heads and went in the pen.

We can learn to control our thoughts in the same way, by gentle determination, not force.

We take an affirmation and repeat it continually, while our thoughts are on the rampage.

We cannot always control our thoughts, but we *can control our words*, and repetition impresses the subconscious, and we are then master of the situation.

In the sixth chapter of Jeremiah we read: "I set a watchman over you, saying, Hearken to the sound of the trumpet."

Your success and happiness in life depend upon the watchman at the gate of your thoughts, for your thoughts, sooner or later, crystallize on the external.

People think by running away from a negative situation, they will be rid of it, but the same situation confronts them wherever they go.

They will meet the same experiences until they have learned their lessons. This idea is brought out in the moving picture, "The Wizard of Oz."

The little girl, Dorothy, is very unhappy because the mean woman in the village wants to take away her dog, Toto.

She goes, in despair, to confide in her Aunt Em and Uncle Henry, but they are too busy to listen, and tell her to "run along."

She says to Toto, "There is somewhere, a wonderful place high above the skies where everybody is happy and no one is mean." How she would love to be there!

A Kansas cyclone suddenly comes along, and she and Toto are lifted up, high in the sky, and land in the country of Oz.

Everything seems very delightful at first, but soon she has the same old experiences. The mean old woman of the village has turned into a terrible witch, and is still trying to get Toto from her.

How she wishes she were back in Kansas.

She is told to find the Wizard of Oz. He is all powerful and will grant her request.

She starts off to find his palace in the Emerald City.

On the way she meets a scarecrow. He is so unhappy because he hasn't a brain.

She meets a man made of tin, who is so unhappy because he hasn't a heart.

Then she meets a lion who is so unhappy because he has no courage.

She cheers them up by saying, "We'll all go to the Wizard of Oz and he'll give us what we want"—the scarecrow a brain, the tin man a heart, and the lion courage.

They encounter terrible experiences, for the bad witch is determined to capture Dorothy and take away Toto and the ruby slippers which protect her.

At last they reach the Emerald Palace of the Wizard of Oz.

They ask for an audience, but are told no one has ever seen the Wizard of Oz, who lives mysteriously in the palace.

But through the influence of the good witch of the North, they enter the palace. There they discover that the Wizard is just a fake magician from Dorothy's home town in Kansas.

They are all in despair because their wishes cannot be granted!

But then the good witch shows them that their wishes are *already* granted. The scarecrow has developed a brain by having to decide what to do in the experiences he has encountered, the tin man finds he has a heart because he loves Dorothy, and the lion has become courageous because he *had* to show courage in his many adventures.

The good witch from the North says to Dorothy, "What have you learned from your experiences?" and Dorothy replies, "I have learned that my heart's desire is in my own home and in my own front yard." So the good witch waves her wand, and Dorothy is at home again.

She wakes up and finds that the scarecrow, the tin man, and the lion are the men who work on her uncle's farm. They are so glad to have her back. This story teaches *that if you run away your problems will run after you.*

Be *undisturbed* by a situation, and it will fall away of its own weight.

There is an occult law of indifference. "None of these things moves me." "None of these things disturbs me;" we might say in modern language.

When you can no longer be disturbed, all disturbance will disappear from the external.

"When your eyes have seen your teachers, your teachers disappear."

"I set watchmen over you, saying, Hearken to the sound of the trumpet."

A trumpet is a musical instrument, used in olden times, to draw people's attention to something; to victory, to order.

You will form the habit of giving attention to every thought and word, when you realize their importance.

The imagination, the scissors of the mind, is constantly cutting out the events to come into your life.

Many people are cutting out fear-pictures. Seeing things which are not divinely planned.

With the "single eye," man sees only the Truth. He sees through evil, knowing that out of it comes good. He transmutes injustice into justice, and disarms his seeming enemy by sending *goodwill.*

We read in mythology of the Cyclops, a race of giants, said to have inhabited Sicily. These giants had only one eye in the middle of the forehead.

The seat of the imagining faculty is situated in the forehead (between the eyes). So these fabled giants came from this idea.

You are indeed a giant when you have a single eye. Then every thought will be a constructive thought, and every word, a word of Power.

Let the third eye be the watchman at the gate.

"If therefore thine eye be single, thy whole body is full of light."

With the single eye your body will be transformed into your spiritual body, the "body electric" made in God's likeness and image (imagination).

By seeing clearly the perfect plan, we could redeem the world: with our *inner eye* seeing a world of peace and plenty and good will.

"Judge not by appearances, judge righteous judgment."

"Nation shall not lift up sword against nation, neither shall they learn war anymore."

The occult law of indifference means that you are undisturbed by adverse appearances. You hold steadily to the *constructive thought,* which *wins out.*

Spiritual law transcends the law of Karma.

This is the attitude of mind which must be held by the healer or practitioner towards his patient.

Indifferent to appearances of lack, loss or sickness, he brings about the change in mind, body and affairs.

Let me quote from the thirty-first chapter of Jeremiah. The keynote is one of rejoicing. It gives a picture of the individual freed from negative thinking.

"For there shall be a day that the watchmen upon the mount Ephraim shall cry, Arise ye, and let us go up to Zion unto the Lord our God."

The Watchman at the Gate neither slumbers nor sleeps. It is the "eye which watches over Israel."

But the individual, living in a world of negative thought, is not conscious of this inner eye.

He may occasionally have flashes of intuition or illumination, then falls back into a world of chaos.

It takes determination and eternal vigilance to check up on words and thoughts. Thoughts of fear, failure, resentment and ill-will must be dissolved and dissipated.

Take the statement: "Every plant my father in heaven has not planted shall be rooted up."

This gives you a vivid picture of rooting up weeds in a garden. They are thrown aside, and dry up because they are without soil to nourish them.

You nourish negative thoughts by giving them your attention. Use the occult law of indifference and refuse to be interested.

Soon you will starve out the "army of the aliens." Divine ideas will crowd your consciousness, false ideas fade away, and you will desire only that which God desires through you.

The Chinese have a proverb, "The Philosopher leaves the cut of his coat to the tailor."

So leave the plan of your life to the Divine Designer, and you will find all conditions permanently perfect.

The ground I am on is holy ground. I now expand rapidly into the divine plan of my life, where all conditions are permanently perfect.

THE WAY OF ABUNDANCE

"Then shalt thou lay up gold as dust."—Job 22:24

The way of abundance is a one-way street.

As the old saying is, "there are no two ways about it."

You are either heading for lack, or heading for abundance. The man with a rich consciousness and the man with a poor consciousness are not walking on the same mental street.

There is a lavish supply, divinely planned for each individual.

The rich man is tapping it, for rich thoughts produce rich surroundings.

Change your thoughts, and in the twinkling of an eye, all your conditions change. Your world is a world of crystallized ideas, crystallized words.

Sooner or later, you reap the fruits of your words and thoughts.

"Words are bodies or forces which move spirally and return in due season to cross the lives of their creators." People who are always talking lack and limitation, reap lack and limitation.

You cannot enter the Kingdom of Abundance bemoaning your lot.

I know a woman who had always been limited in her ideas of prosperity. She was continually making her old clothes "do," instead of buying new clothes. She was very careful of what money she had, and was always advising her husband not to spend so much. She said repeatedly, "I don't want anything I can't afford."

She couldn't afford much, so she didn't have much. Suddenly her whole world cracked up. Her husband left her, weary of her nagging and limited thoughts. She was in despair, when one day she came across a book on metaphysics. It explained the power of thought and words.

She realized that she had invited every unhappy experience by wrong thinking. She laughed heartily at her mistakes, and decided to profit by them. She determined *to prove the law of abundance.*

She used what money she had, fearlessly, to show her faith in her invisible supply. She relied upon God as the source of her prosperity. She no longer voiced lack and limitation. She kept herself feeling and looking prosperous.

Her old friends scarcely recognized her. She had swung into the way of abundance. More money came to her than she had ever had before. Unheard-of doors opened—amazing channels were freed. She became very successful in a work she had had no training for.

She found herself on *miracle ground.* What had happened?

She had changed the quality of her words and thoughts. She had taken God into her confidence, and into all her affairs. She had many eleventh-hour demonstrations, but her supply always came, for she dug her ditches and gave thanks without wavering.

Someone called me up recently and said, "I am looking desperately for a position."

I replied, "Don't look desperately for it, look for it with praise and thanksgiving, for Jesus Christ, the greatest of metaphysicians, said to pray with praise and thanksgiving."

Praise and thanksgiving open the gates, for expectancy always wins.

Of course, the law is impersonal, and a dishonest person with rich thoughts will attract riches—but, "a thing ill-got has ever bad success," as Shakespeare says. It will be of short duration and will not bring happiness.

We have only to read the papers to see that the way of the transgressor is hard.

That is the reason it is so necessary to make your demands aright on the Universal Supply, and ask for what is yours by divine right and under grace in a perfect way.

Some people attract prosperity, but cannot hold it. Sometimes their heads are turned, sometimes they lose it through fear and worry.

A friend in one of my question and answer classes told this story.

Some people in his home town, who had always been poor, suddenly struck oil in their back yard. It brought great riches. The father joined the country club and went in for golf. He was no longer young—the exercise was too much for him and he dropped dead on the links.

This filled the whole family with fear. They all decided they might have heart trouble, so they are now in bed with trained nurses watching every heart beat.

In the race-thought people must worry about something.

They no longer worried about money, so they shifted their worries to health.

The old idea was, "that you can't have everything." If you got one thing, you'd lose another. People were always saying, "Your luck won't last," "It's too good to be true."

Jesus Christ said, "In the world (world thought) there is tribulation, but be of good cheer, I have overcome the world (thought)."

In the superconscious (or Christ within), there is a lavish supply for every demand, and your good is perfect and permanent.

"If thou return to the Almighty, thou shalt be built up (in consciousness), thou shalt put away iniquity far from thy tabernacles."

"Then shalt thou lay up gold as dust, the gold of Ophir as the stones of the brooks."

"Yea, the Almighty shall be thy defense and thou shalt have plenty of silver."

What a picture of opulence! The result of "Returning to the Almighty (in consciousness)."

With the average person (who has thought in terms of lack for a long time) it is very difficult to build up a rich consciousness.

I have a student who has attracted great success by making the statement: "*I am the daughter of the King! My rich Father now pours out his abundance upon me: I am the daughter of the King! Everything makes way for me.*"

Many people put up with limited conditions because they are too lazy (mentally), to think themselves out of them.

You must have a great desire for financial freedom, you must feel yourself rich, you must see yourself rich, you must continually prepare for riches. Become as a little child and make believe you are rich. You are then impressing the subconscious with expectancy.

The imagination is man's workshop, the scissors of the mind, where he is constantly cutting out the events of his life!

The superconscious is the realm of inspiration, revelation, illumination and intuition.

Intuition is usually known as a hunch. I do not apologize for the word "hunch" anymore. It is now in Webster's latest dictionary.

I had a hunch to look up "hunch," and there it was.

The superconscious is the realm of perfect ideas. The great genius captures his thoughts from the superconscious.

"Without the vision (imagination) my people perish."

When people have lost the power to image their good, they "perish" (or go under).

It is interesting to compare the translation of the French and English Bibles. In the 21st verse of the 22nd chapter of Job we read: "Acquaint now thyself with him, and be at peace: thereby good shall come unto thee." In the French Bible we read: "Attach thyself to God and you will have peace. Thou shalt thus enjoy happiness."

The 23rd verse: "If thou return to the Almighty, thou shalt be built up, thou shalt put away iniquity far from thy tabernacles." In the French translation we read: "Thou shalt be re-established if thou returnest to the Almighty, putting iniquity far off from your dwellings."

In the 24th verse we read a new and amazing translation. The English Bible reads: "Then shalt thou lay up gold as dust, and the gold of Ophir as the stones of the brooks." The French Bible says: "Throw gold into the dust, the gold of Ophir amongst the pebbles of the torrents; and the Almighty shall be thy gold, thy silver, thy riches."

This means if people are depending entirely on their visible supply, it is even better to throw it away and trust absolutely to the Almighty for gold, silver and riches.

I give an example in the story told me by a friend.

A priest went to visit a nunnery in France, where they fed many children. One of the nuns, in despair, told the priest they had no food; the children must go hungry. She said that they had but one piece of silver (about the value of a quarter of a dollar). They needed food and clothing. The priest said, "Give me the coin."

She handed it to him and he threw it out the window.

"Now," he said, "rely entirely upon God." Within a short time friends arrived with plenty of food and gifts of money. This does not mean to throw away what money you have, but don't depend upon it. Depend upon your invisible supply, the Bank of the Imagination.

Let us now attach ourselves to God and have peace. For He shall be our gold, our silver and our riches.

The inspiration of the Almighty shall be my defense and I shall have plenty of silver.

I SHALL NEVER WANT

"The Lord is my Shepherd; I shall not want."—Psalms 23:1

The 23rd Psalm is the best known of all the Psalms—we might say that it is the keynote to the message of the Bible.

It tells man he shall never want, when he has the realization (or conviction) that the Lord is his Shepherd: the *realization* that Infinite Intelligence supplies every need.

If you get this conviction today, every need will be met now and forever-more; you will draw, instantly, from the abundance of the spheres, whatever you desire or require; for what you need is *already on your pathway.*

A woman suddenly had the realization: "The Lord is my Shepherd, I shall never want." She seemed to be touching her invisible supply, she felt outside of Time and Space, she no longer relied on the external.

Her first demonstration was a small, but necessary one. She needed at once, some large paperclips, but had no time to go to a stationer's to buy them.

In looking for something else, she opened a little-used chest, and in it, she found, about a dozen large paper-clips.

She felt that the law was working, and gave thanks; then some needed money appeared, things large and small came her way.

Since then she has relied upon the statement: "The Lord is my Shepherd, I shall never want."

We used to hear people say, "I do not think it is right to ask God for money or things."

They did not realize that this Creative Principle is within each man.—(The Father within). True Spirituality is proving God as your supply, daily—not just once in a while.

Jesus Christ knew this law, for whatever He desired or required, appeared immediately on His pathway, the loaves and fishes and money from the fish's mouth.

With this realization, all hoarding and saving would disappear.

This does not mean that you should not have a big bank account, and investments, but it does mean that you should not depend upon them, for if you had a loss in one direction, you would have a gain in another.

Always "your barns would be full and your cup flow over."

Now, how does one make this contact with his invisible supply? By taking a statement of Truth which clicks and gives him realization.

This is not open to a chosen few, "Whosoever calleth on the name of the Lord shall be delivered." The Lord is *your* shepherd and *my* shepherd and everybody's shepherd.

God is the Supreme Intelligence devoted to supplying man's need; the explanation is, that man is God in action. Jesus Christ said, "I and the Father are one.

We might paraphrase the statement and say, I and the great Creative Principle of the Universe, are one and the same.

Man only lacks when he loses his contact with this Creative Principle, which must be fully trusted, for it is Pure Intelligence and knows the way of Fulfillment.

The reasoning mind and personal will, cause a short circuit.

"Trust in me and I will bring it to pass."

Most people are filled with apprehension and dread, when there is nothing to cling to on the external.

A woman came to a practitioner and said, "I'm only a poor little woman with no one but God back of me." The practitioner said, - "You need not worry if you have God back of you," for "all that the Kingdom affords is yours."

A woman called me on the phone and said, almost in tears, "I'm so worried about the business situation." I replied, "The situation with God remains the same: The Lord is your Shepherd: you shall not want." "If one door shuts, another door opens."

A very successful business-man who conducts all affairs on Truth methods, said, "The trouble with most people is, that they get to relying on certain conditions. They haven't enough imagination to go forward—to open new channels."

Nearly every big success is built upon a failure.

I was told that Edgar Bergen lost his part in a Broadway production because they did not want any more dummies. Noel Coward got him on the Rudy Vallee radio hour, and he and Charlie McCarthy became famous over night.

I told the story, at one of my meetings, of a man who was so poor and discouraged, that he ended it all. A few days later, came a letter notifying him that he had inherited a large fortune.

A man in the meeting said: "That means, when you want to be dead, your demonstration is three days off." Yes, *do not be fooled by the darkness before the dawn.*

It is a good thing to see the dawn once in a while, to convince you how unfailing it is. It reminds me of an experience of several years ago.

I had a friend who lived in Brooklyn near Prospect Park. She liked to do unusual things and said to me: "Come to visit me and we'll get up early and see the sun-rise in Prospect Park."

At first I refused, and then came the hunch that it would be an interesting experience.

It was in the summer. We got up about four o'clock,—my friend, her little daughter and myself. It was pitch dark, but we sallied forth down the street, to the entrance of the Park.

Some policemen eyed us curiously, but my friend said to them with dignity, "We are going to see the sun-rise;" and it seemed to satisfy them. We walked through the Park to the beautiful rose-garden.

A faint pink streak appeared in the East, then suddenly, we heard a most tremendous uproar. We were near the Zoo and all the animals were greeting the dawn.

The lions and tigers roared, the hyenas laughed, there were shrieks and howls: every animal had something to say, for a new day was at hand.

It was indeed, most inspiring. The light slanted through the trees; everything had an unearthly aspect.

Then, as it grew lighter, our shadows were in front instead of behind us. The dawn of a new day!

This is the wonderful dawn which comes to each one of us, after some darkness.

Your dawn of Success, Happiness and Abundance is sure to come.

Every day is important, for we read in the wonderful Sanskrit poem, "Look well, therefore, to this day, such is the salutation of the dawn."

This day the Lord is your Shepherd! This day, you shall not want; as you and this great Creative Principle are one and the same.

The 34th Psalm is also a Psalm of security. It starts with a blessing for the Lord, "I will bless the Lord at all times: His praise shall continually be in my mouth."

"They that seek the Lord shall not want any good thing." Seeking the Lord means that man must make the first move. "Draw near to me and I will draw near to thee, saith the Lord."

You seek the Lord by making your affirmation, expecting and preparing for your good.

If you ask for success and prepare for failure, you will receive the thing you have prepared for.

I tell in my book, "The Game of Life and How to Play It," of a man who asked me to speak the word that all his debts be wiped out.

After the treatment, he said, "Now I'm thinking what I'll say to the people when I haven't the money to pay them." A treatment won't help you if you haven't faith in it, for faith and expectancy impress the subconscious mind with the picture of fulfillment.

In the 23rd Psalm we read, "He restoreth my soul." Your soul is your subconscious mind and must be re-stored with the right ideas.

Whatever you feel deeply is impressed upon the subconscious, and manifests in your affairs.

If you are convinced that you are a failure, you will be a failure, until you impress the subconscious with the conviction you are a success.

This is done by making an affirmation which "clicks."

A friend in a meeting said that I had given her the statement as she was leaving the room - "*The ground you are on is harvest ground.*" Things with her, had been very dull; but this statement clicked.

"*Harvest Ground, Harvest Ground,*" rang in her ears. Good things immediately commenced to come to her, and happy surprises.

The reason it is necessary to make an affirmation is because repetition impresses the subconscious. You cannot control your thoughts at first, but you can control your words, and Jesus Christ said: "By your *words* you are justified and by your words you are condemned."

Every day, choose the right words; the right thoughts! The Imaging faculty is the creative faculty: "Out of the imaginations of the heart come the issues of life."

We have all a bank we can draw upon, the Bank of the Imagination.

Let us imagine ourselves rich, well and happy: imagine all our affairs in divine order; but leave the way of fulfillment to Infinite Intelligence.

"He has weapons ye know not of," He has channels which will surprise you.

One of the most important passages in the 23rd Psalm is - "Thou preparest a table before me in the presence of mine enemies."

This means that even in the presence of the enemy situation, brought on by your doubts, fears or resentments, a way out is prepared for you.

The Lord is my Shepherd; I shall never want.

LOOK WITH WONDER

"I will remember the works of the Lord; surely I will remember thy wonders of old."—Psalms 77:11

The words wonder and wonderful are used many times in the Bible. In the dictionary the word wonder is defined as, "a cause for surprise, astonishment, a miracle, a marvel."

Ouspensky, in his book, "Tertium Organum," calls the 4th dimensional world, the "World of the Wondrous." He has figured out mathematically, that there is a realm where all conditions are perfect. Jesus Christ called it the Kingdom.

We might say, "Seek ye first the world of the wondrous, and all things shall be added unto you."

It can only be reached through a state of consciousness.

Jesus Christ said, to enter the Kingdom, we must become "as a little child." Children are continually in a state of joy and wonder!

The future holds promises of mysterious good. Anything can happen over night.

Robert Louis Stevenson, in "A Child's Garden of Verses" says: "The world is so full of a number of things, I'm sure we should all be as happy as kings."

So let us look with wonder at that which is before us; that statement was given me a number of years ago, I mention it in my book, "The Game of Life and How To Play It."

I had missed an opportunity and felt that I should have been more awake to my good. The next day, I took the statement early in the morning, "I look with wonder at that which is before me."

At noon the phone rang, and the proposition was put to me again. This time I grasped it: I did indeed, look with wonder for I never expected the opportunity to come to me again.

A friend in one of my meetings said the other day, that this statement had brought her wonderful results. It fills the consciousness with happy expectancy.

Children are filled with happy expectancy until grown-up people, and unhappy experiences bring them out of the world of the wondrous!

Let us look back and remember some of the gloomy ideas which were given us: "Eat the speckled apples first." "Don't expect too much, then you won't be disappointed." "You can't have everything in this life." "Childhood is your happiest time." "No one knows what the future will bring." What a start in life!

These are some of the impressions I picked up in early childhood.

At the age of six I had a great sense of responsibility. Instead of looking with wonder at that which was before me,

I looked with fear and suspicion. I feel much younger now than I did when I was six.

I have an early photograph taken about that time, grasping a flower, but with a careworn and hopeless expression.

I had left the world of the wondrous behind me! I was now living in the world of realities, as my elders told me, and it was far from wondrous.

It is a great privilege for children to live in this age, when they are taught Truth from their birth. Even if they are not taught actual metaphysics, the ethers are filled with joyous expectancy.

You may become a Shirley Temple or a Freddy Bartholomew or a great pianist at the age of six, and go on a concert tour.

We are all now, back in the world of the wondrous, where anything can happen over-night, for when miracles do come, they come quickly!

So let us become *Miracle Conscious:* prepare for miracles, expect miracles, and we are then inviting them into our lives.

Maybe you need a financial miracle! There is a supply for every demand. Through active faith, the word, and intuition, we release this invisible supply.

I will give an example: One of my students found herself almost without funds, she needed one thousand dollars, and she had had plenty of money at one time and beautiful possessions, but had nothing left but an ermine wrap. No fur dealer would give her much for it.

I spoke the word that it would be sold to the right person for the right price, or that the supply would come in some other way. It was necessary that the money manifest at once, it was no time to worry or reason.

She was on the street making her affirmations. It was a stormy day—She said to herself, "I'm going to show active faith in my invisible supply by taking a taxi cab:" it was a very strong hunch. As she got out of the taxi, at her destination, a woman stood waiting to get in.

It was an old friend: a very very kind friend. It was the first time in her life she had ever taken a taxi, but her Rolls Royce was out of commission that afternoon.

They talked, and my friend told her about the ermine wrap; "Why," her friend said, "I will give you a thousand dollars for it." And that afternoon she had the cheque.

God's ways are ingenious, His methods are sure.

A student wrote me the other day, that she was using that statement—*God's ways are ingenious, His methods are sure.* A series of unexpected contacts brought about a situation she had been desiring. She looked with wonder at the working of the law.

Our demonstrations usually come within a "split second." All is timed with amazing accuracy in Divine Mind.

My student left the taxi, just as her friend stopped to enter; a second later, she would have hailed another taxi.

Man's part is to be wide awake to his leads and hunches; for on the magic path of Intuition is all that he desires or requires.

In Moulton's Modern Reader's Bible, the book of Psalms is recognized as the perfection of lyric poetry.

"The musical meditation which is the essence of lyrics can find no higher field than the devout spirit which at once raises itself to the service of God, and overflows on the various sides of active and contemplative life."

The Psalms are also human documents, and I have selected the 77th Psalm because it gives the picture of a man in despair, but as he contemplates the wonders of God, faith and assurance are restored to him.

"I cried unto God with my voice, even unto God with my voice; and He gave ear unto me.

In the day of my trouble I sought the Lord: my soul refused to be comforted.

Will the Lord cast off forever? and will he be favourable no more?

Hath God forgotten to be gracious? hath he in anger shut up his tender mercies?

And I said, This is my infirmity: but I will remember the years of the right hand of the Most High.

I will remember the works of the Lord; surely I will remember thy wonders of old.

I will meditate also of all thy work, and talk of thy doings.

Thy way, O God, is in the sanctuary: who is so great a God as our God!

Thou art the God that doest wonders.

Thou hast with thine arm redeemed thy people."

This is a picture of what the average Truth student goes through, when confronted with a problem; he is assailed by thoughts of doubt, fear and despair.

Then some statement of Truth will flash into his consciousness - "God's ways are ingenious, His methods are sure!" He remembers other difficulties which have been overcome, his confidence in God returns. He thinks, "*what God has done before, He will do for me and more!*"

I was talking to a friend not long ago who said: "I would be pretty dumb if I didn't believe God could solve my problem. So many times before, wonderful things have come to me, I know they will come again!"

So the summing up of the 77th Psalm is, "What God has done before, He now does for me and more!"

It is a good thing to say when you think of your past success, happiness or wealth: all loss comes from your own vain imaginings, fear of loss crept into your consciousness, you carried burdens and fought battles, you reasoned instead of sticking to the magic path of intuition.

But in the twinkling of an eye, all will be restored to you—for as they say in the East - "What Allah has given, cannot be diminished."

Now to go back to the child's state of consciousness, you should be filled with wonder, but be careful not to live in your past childhood.

I know people who can only think about their happy childhood days: they remember what they wore! No skies have since been so blue, or grass so green. They therefore miss the opportunities of the wonderful now.

I will tell an amusing story of a friend who lived in a town when she was very young, then moved away to another city. She always looked back to the house they first lived in; to her it was an enchanted palace: large, spacious and glamorous.

Many years after, when she had grown up, she had an opportunity of visiting this house. She was disillusioned: she found it small, stuffy and ugly. Her idea of beauty had entirely changed, for in the front yard was an iron dog.

If you went back to your past, it would not be the same. So in this friend's family, they called living in the past, "iron-dogging."

Her sister told me a story of some "iron-dogging" she had done. When she was about sixteen, she met abroad, a very dashing and romantic young man, an artist. This romance didn't last long, but she talked about it a lot to the man she afterwards married. Years rolled by, the dashing and romantic young man, had become a well-known artist, and came to this country to have an exhibition of his pictures. My friend was filled with excitement, and hunted him up to renew their friendship. She went to his exhibition, and in walked a portly business man—no trace was left of the dashing romantic youth! When she told her husband, all he said was, "iron-dogging."

Remember, *now* is the appointed time! *Today* is the day! *And your good can happen over night.*

Look with wonder at that which is before you!

We are filled with divine expectancy: "I will restore to you the years which the locusts have eaten!"

Now let each one think of the good which seems so difficult to attain; it may be health, wealth, happiness or perfect self-expression. Do not think *how* your good can be accomplished, just give thanks that you have already received on the invisible plane, "therefore the steps leading up to it are secured also."

Be wide awake to your intuitive leads, and suddenly, you find yourself in your Promised Land.

"I look with wonder at that which is before me."

CATCH UP WITH YOUR GOOD

> "And it shall come to pass, that before they call, I will answer: and while they are yet speaking, I will hear."
>
> —Isaiah 65:24

Catch up with your good! This is a new way of saying, "Before they call, I will answer."

Your good *precedes* you; it gets there before you do. But how to catch up with your good? For you must have ears that hear, and eyes that see, or it will escape you.

Some people never catch up with their good in life; they will say, "My life has always been one of hardship, no good luck ever comes to me." They are the people who have been asleep to their opportunities; or through laziness, haven't caught up with their good.

A woman told a group of friends that she had not eaten for three days. They dashed about asking people to give her work; but she refused it. She explained that she never got up until twelve o'clock, she liked to lie in bed and read magazines.

She just wanted people to support her while she read "Vogue" and "Harper's Bazaar." We must be careful not to slip into lazy states of mind. Take the affirmation, *I am wide awake to my good, I never miss a trick*. Most people are only half awake to their good.

A student said to me, "If I don't follow my hunches, I always get into a jam."

I will tell the story of a woman, one of my students, who followed her intuitive lead, which brought amazing results.

She had been asked to visit friends in a nearby town. She had very little money. When she arrived at her destination, she found the house locked up, they had gone away: she was filled with despair, then commenced to pray: she said, "Infinite Intelligence, give me a definite lead, let me know just what to do!"

The name of a certain hotel flashed into her consciousness—it persisted—the name seemed to stand out in big letters.

She had just enough money to get back to New York and the hotel. As she was about to enter, an old friend suddenly appeared, who greeted her warmly; and whom she hadn't seen for years.

She explained that she was living at the hotel but was going away for several months, and added, "Why don't you live in my suite while I am away:—it won't cost you a cent."

My friend accepted gratefully, and looked with amazement on the working of Spiritual law.

She had caught up with her good by following intuition.

All going forward comes from desire. Science today, is going back to Lamarck and his "dint—of wishing" theory. He claims that birds do not fly because they have wings, but they have wings because they wanted to fly; result of the "Push of the emotional wish."

Think of the irresistible power of thought with clear vision. Many people are in a fog most of the time, making wrong decisions and going the wrong way.

During the Christmas rush, my maid said to a saleswoman at one of the big shops, "I suppose this is your busiest day." She replied, "Oh no! the day *after* Christmas is our busiest day, when people bring most of the things back."

Hundreds of people choosing the wrong gifts because they were not listening to their intuitive leads.

No matter what you are doing, ask for guidance. It saves time and energy and often a lifetime of misery.

All suffering comes from the violation of intuition. Unless intuition builds the house, they labor in vain who build it.

Get the *habit of hunching*, then you will always be on the magic path.

"And it shall come to pass, that before they call, I will answer: and while they are yet speaking, I will hear."

Working with spiritual law, we are bringing to pass that which already is. In the Universal Mind it is there as an idea, but is crystallized on the external, by a sincere desire.

The idea of a bird was a perfect picture in divine mind; the fish caught the idea, and wished themselves into birds.

Are your desires bringing you wings? *We should all be bringing some seemingly impossible thing to pass.*

One of my affirmations is, "*The unexpected happens, my seemingly impossible good now comes to pass.*"

Do not magnify obstacles, magnify the Lord—that means, magnify God's power.

The average person will dwell on all the obstacles and hindrances which are there to prevent his good coming to pass.

You "combine with what you notice," so if you give obstacles and hindrances your undivided attention, they grow worse and worse.

Give God your undivided attention. Keep saying silently (in the face of all obstacles), "*God's ways are ingenious, His methods are sure.*"

God's power is invincible, (though invisible). "Call unto me and I will answer thee, and show thee great and mighty things, which thou knowest not."

In demonstrating our good, we must look away from adverse appearances, "Judge not by appearances."

Get some statement which will give you a feeling of assurance, *The long arm of God reaches out over people and conditions, controlling the situation and protecting my interests!*

I was asked to speak the word for a man who was to have a business interview with a seemingly unscrupulous person. I used the statement, and rightness and justice came out of the situation, at just the exact time I was speaking.

We have all heard the quotation from Proverbs, "Hope deferred maketh the heart grow sick, but when the desire cometh, it is a tree of life."

In desiring sincerely (without anxiety), we are catching up with the thing desired; and the desire becomes crystallized on the external. "I will give to you the rightous desires of your heart."

Selfish desires, desires which harm others, always return to harm the sender.

The righteous desire might be called, an echo from the Infinite. It is already a perfect idea in divine mind.

All inventors catch up with the ideas of the articles they invent. I say in my book, "The Game of Life and How To Play It," the telephone was seeking Bell.

Often two people discover the same inventions at the same time; they have tuned in with the same idea.

The most important thing in life, is to bring the divine plan to pass.

Just as the picture of the oak is in the acorn, the divine design of your life is in your superconscious mind, and you must work out the perfect pattern in your affairs. You will then lead a magic life, for in the divine design, all conditions are permanently perfect.

People defy the divine design when they are asleep to their good.

Perhaps the woman who liked to lie in bed most of the day, and read magazines, should be writing for magazines, but her habits of laziness dulled all desire to go forward.

The fishes who desired wings, were alert and alive, they did not spend their days on the bed of the ocean, reading "Vogue" and "Harper's Bazaar."

Awake thou that sleepeth and catch up with your good!

"Call on me and I will answer thee, and show thee great and mighty things, which thou knowest not."

I now catch up with my good, for before I called I was answered.

RIVERS IN THE DESERT

> "Behold, I will do a new thing: now it shall spring forth; shall ye not know it? I will even make a way in the wilderness, and rivers in the desert."—Isaiah 43:19.

In this 43rd chapter of Isaiah, are many wonderful statements, showing the irresistible power of Supreme Intelligence, coming to man's rescue in times of trouble. *No matter how impossible the situation seems, Infinite Intelligence knows the way out.*

Working with God-Power, man becomes unconditioned and absolute. Let us get a realization of this hidden power we can call upon at any moment.

Make your contact with Infinite Intelligence, (the God within) and all appearance of evil evaporates, for it comes from man's "vain imaginings."

In my question and answer class I would be asked, "How do you make a conscious contract with this Invincible Power?"

I reply, "By your word." "By your word you are justified."

The Centurion said to Jesus Christ, "Speak the word master and my servant shall be healed."

"Whosoever calleth on the name of the Lord shall be delivered." Notice the word, "call:" you are calling on the Lord or Law, when you make an affirmation of Truth.

As I always say, take a statement which "clicks," that means, gives you a feeling of security.

People are enslaved by ideas of lack; lack of love, lack of money, lack of companionship, lack of health, and so on.

They are enslaved by the ideas of interference and incompletion. They are asleep in the Adamic Dream: Adam (generic man,) ate of "Maya the tree of illusion" and saw two powers, good and evil.

The Christ mission was to wake people up to the Truth of one Power, God. "Awake thou that sleepeth."

If you lack any good thing, you are still asleep to your good.

How do you awake from the Adamic dream of opposites, after having slept soundly in the race thought for hundreds of years?

Jesus Christ said, "When two of you agree, it shall be done." It is the law of agreement.

It is almost impossible to see clearly, your good, for yourself: that is where the healer, practitioner or friend is necessary.

Many successful men say they have succeeded because their wives believed in them. -

I will quote from a current newspaper, giving Walter P. Chrysler's tribute to his wife: "Nothing," he once said, "has given me more satisfaction in life, than the way my wife had faith in me from the very first, through all those years." Chrysler wrote of her, "It seemed to me I could not make any one understand that I was ambitious except Della. I could tell her and she would nod. It seems to me I even dared to tell her that I intended, some day, to be master mechanic." She always backed his ambitions.

Talk about your affairs as little as possible, and then only to the ones who will give you encouragement and inspiration. The world is full of "Wet blankets," people who tell you "it can't be done," that you are aiming too high..

As people sit in Truth meetings and services, often a word or an idea will open a way in the wilderness.

Of course the Bible is speaking of states of consciousness. You are in a wilderness or desert, when you are out of harmony—when you are angry, resentful, fearful or undecided. Indecision is the cause of much ill health, being unable "to make up your mind."

One day when I was in a bus, a woman stopped it and asked the conductor its destination. He told her, but she was undecided. She got half way on, and then got off, then on again: the conductor turned to her and said, "Lady make up your mind!"

So it is with so many people: "Ladies make up your minds!"

The intuitive person is never undecided: he is given his leads and hunches, and goes boldly ahead, knowing he is on the magic path.

In Truth, we always ask for definite leads just what to do; you will always receive one if you ask for it. Sometimes it comes as intuition, sometimes from the external.

One of my students, named Ada, was walking down the street, undecided whether to go to a certain place, or not; she asked for a lead. Two women were walking in front of her.

One turned to the other and said, "Why don't you go Ada?"—The woman's name just happened to be Ada—my friend took it as a definite lead, and went on to her destination, and the outcome was very successful.

We really lead magic lives, guided and provided for at every step; *if we have ears to hear and eyes that see.*

Of course we have left the plane of the intellect and are drawing from the superconscious, the God within, which says, "This is the way, walk ye in it."

Whatever you should know, will be revealed to you. Whatever you lack, will be provided! "Thus saith the Lord which maketh a way in the sea and a path in the mighty waters."

"Remember ye not the former things, neither consider the things of old."

People who live in the past have severed their contact with the wonderful now. God knows only the now; now is the appointed time, today is the day.

Many people lead lives of limitation, hoarding and saving, afraid to use what they have; which brings more lack and more limitation.

I give the example of a woman who lived in a small country town: she could scarcely see to get about, and had very little money. A kind friend took her to an oculist, and presented her with glasses, which enabled her to see perfectly. Sometime later she met her on the street without the glasses. She exclaimed, "Where are your glasses?"

The woman replied, "Well, you don't expect me to hack 'em out by using them every day, do you? I only wear them on Sundays."

You must live in the now and be wide awake to your opportunities.

"Behold, I will do a new thing: now it shall spring forth; shall ye not know it? I will even make a way in the wilderness, and rivers in the desert."

This message is meant for the individual: think of your problem and know that Infinite Intelligence knows the way of fulfillment. I say the *way*, for before you called you were answered. *The supply always precedes the demand.*

God is the Giver and the Gift and now creates His own amazing channels.

When you have asked for the Divine Plan of your life to manifest, you are protected from getting the things that are not in the Divine Plan.

You may think that all your happiness depends upon obtaining one particular thing in life; later on, you praise the Lord that you didn't get it.

Sometimes you are tempted to follow the reasoning mind, and argue with your intuitive leads, suddenly the Hand of Destiny pushes you into your right place; under grace, you find yourself back on the magic path again.

You are now wide awake to your good—you have the ears that hear (your intuitive leads,) and the eyes which see the open road of fulfillment.

The genius within me is released. I now fulfill my destiny.

THE INNER MEANING OF SNOW WHITE AND THE SEVEN DWARFS

I have been asked to give a Metaphysical interpretation of Snow White and the Seven Dwarfs, one of Grimm's Fairy Tales.

It is amazing how this picture, a fairy story, swept sophisticated New York, and the whole country, due to Walt Disney's genius.

This fairy tale was supposed to be for children, but men and women have packed the theatre. It is because fairy tales come down from old legends of Persia, India and Egypt, which are founded on Truth.

Snow White, the little Princess, has a cruel stepmother, who is jealous of her. This cruel stepmother idea appeal also in "Cinderella."

Nearly everyone has a cruel step-mother. THE CRUEL STEP-MOTHER IS A NEGATIVE THOUGHT-FORM YOU HAVE BUILT UP IN THE SUBCONSCIOUS.

Snow White's cruel step-mother is jealous of her and always keeps her in rags and in the background.

ALL CRUEL THOUGHT FORMS DO THIS.

The cruel step-mother consults her magic mirror every day, saying: "Magic mirror on the wall, who is the fairest of them all?" One day the mirror replies: "Thou Queen, mayst fair and beauteous be, but Snow White is lovelier far than thee." This enrages the Queen, so she decides to send Snow White to the forest to be killed by one of her servants. However, the servant's heart melts when Snow White begs for her life, so he leaves her in the woods. The woods are filled with terrifying animals and many pitfalls and dangers. She falls in terror to the ground, and while there, a most unusual spectacle presents itself. Scores of the most delightful little animals and birds creep up and surround her. Rabbits, squirrels, deer, beavers, raccoons, etc. She opens her eyes and greets them with pleasure; they are so friendly and attractive. She tells her story and they lead her to a little house which she makes her home. NOW THESE FRIENDLY BIRDS AND ANIMALS SYMBOLIZE OUR INTUITIVE LEADS OR HUNCHES, WHICH ARE ALWAYS READY TO "GET YOU OUT OF THE WOODS."

The little house proves to be the home of the Seven Dwarfs. Everything is in disorder, so Snow White and her animal friends begin to clean the house. The squirrels dust with their tails, the birds hang things up, using the little deer's horns for a hat-rack. When the seven dwarfs come home from their work of digging gold, they discover the change and at last find Snow White asleep on one of the beds. In the morning she tells her story, remains with them to keep house and cook their meals, and is very happy. THE SEVEN DWARFS SYMBOLIZE THE PROTECTIVE FORCES ALL ABOUT US.

In the meantime, the cruel step-mother consults her mirror and it says to her: "Over the hills in the green wood shade, where the Seven Dwarfs their dwelling have made, there Snow White is hiding her head, and she, is lovelier far, Oh, Queen than thee." This infuriates the Queen; so she starts off disguised as an old hag, with a poisoned apple for Snow White. She finds her in the house of the Seven Dwarfs and tempts her with the big, red luscious apple. The birds and animals endeavor to tell her not to touch it. THEY TRY TO GIVE HER THE HUNCH NOT TO EAT IT. They rush around in dismay, but Snow White can't resist the apple, she takes one bite and falls, apparently dead. Now all the little birds and animals rush off to bring the Seven Dwarfs to the rescue; but too late, Snow White lies lifeless. They all bow their little heads in grief. Then suddenly the Prince appears, kisses Snow White, and she comes to life. They are married and live happily ever after. The Queen, the cruel step-mother, is swept away by a terrific storm, THE OLD THOUGHT-FORM IS DISSOLVED AND DISSIPATED FOREVER. THE PRINCE SYMBOLIZES THE DIVINE PLAN OF YOUR LIFE. WHEN IT WAKES YOU UP YOU LIVE HAPPILY EVER AFTER.

This is the fairy story which has enthralled New York and the whole country.

Find out what form of tyranny your cruel stepmother is taking in your subconscious. It is some negative conviction which works out in all your affairs.

We hear people saying: "My good always comes to me too late." "I've lost so many opportunities!" We must reverse the thought and say repeatedly: "*I am wide awake to my good, I never miss a trick.*"

WE MUST DROWN OUT THE DREARY SUGGESTIONS OF THE CRUEL STEPMOTHER. *ETERNAL VIGILANCE IS THE PRICE OF FREEDOM FROM THESE NEGATIVE THOUGHT-FORMS.*

Nothing can hinder, nothing can delay the manifestation of the Divine Plan of my life.
The Light of Lights streams on my pathway, revealing the Open Road of Fulfillment!